Little Scientists®

A "hands-on" approach to learning

Fun With
Water and Bubbles

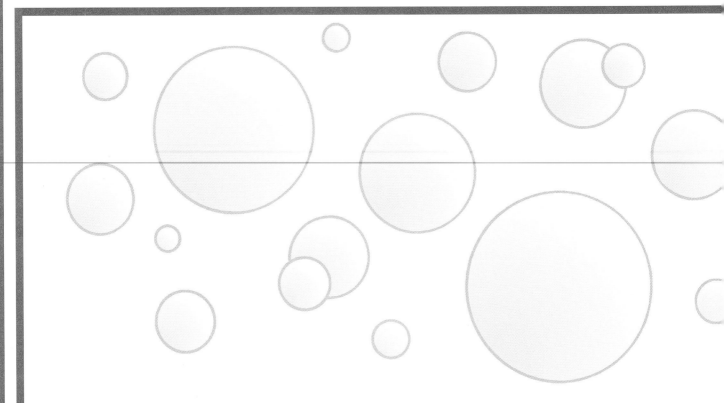

Dear Parents,

Young children are natural scientists, curious about the world around them. They have an infinite capacity to learn and are eager to know why and how things work the way they do. Little Scientists, Hands-On Activities begins with the simple questions most children ask and then shows them how to explore and find out for themselves. Our acclaimed Little Scientists, "hands-on" approach instills in children a passion for the exciting world of science and helps children develop specific scientific skills that will provide a strong foundation for later learning.

With this book, you can join me on a journey into the wonders of Water and Bubbles. Together we will discover the unlocked secrets of water and learn how to create bubbles, clouds, and many other exciting things.

Your Little Scientist can email me at
Dr_Heidi@Little-Scientists.com

Wishing you success,

Dr. Heidi

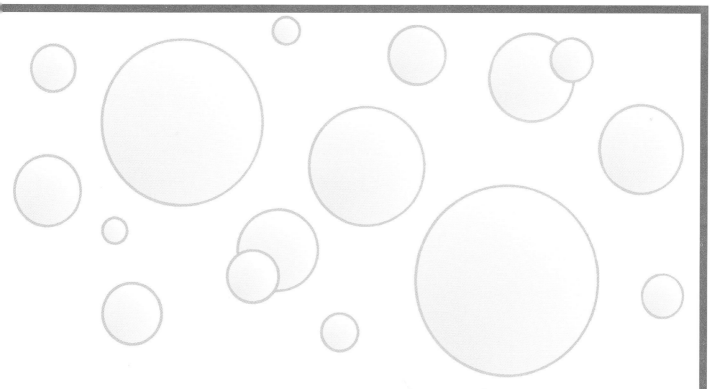

Little Scientists®

A "hands-on" approach to learning

Fun With
Water and Bubbles

Heidi Gold-Dworkin, Ph.D.

McGraw-Hill

New York   San Francisco   Washington, D.C.
Auckland   Bogotá   Caracas   Lisbon   London   Madrid   Mexico City
Milan   Montreal   New Delhi   San Juan   Singapore   Sydney   Tokyo   Toronto

This book is dedicated to my children
Aviva, Olivia, and Robert

This book would not have been possible
without the contributions from the following
staff members at Little Scientists:®
June Stevens
Melissa Dailey
Meredith Girard
Bec Luty
Larry Russick
Linda Burian
Avi Ornstein

McGraw-Hill
*A Division of The **McGraw-Hill** Companies*

pbk   4 5 6 7 8 9 QPD / QPD 9 0 9 8 7 6 5 4 3 2 1

ISBN 0-07-134823-9

Library of Congress Cataloging-in-Publication data applied for.

McGraw-Hill books are available at special quantity discounts to use as premiums
and sales promotions. For more information, please write to the Director of Sales,
McGraw-Hill, 11 West 19th Street, New York, NY 10011. Or contact your local bookstore.

Acquisitions editor: Mary Loebig Giles
Senior Editing Supervisor: Patricia V. Amoroso
Senior production supervisor: Clare B. Stanley
Left page illustrations: Robert K. Ullman <r.k.ullman@worldnet.att.net>
Right page illustrations: K. Almadingen <dzbersin@aol.com>
Book design: Jaclyn J. Boone <bookdesign@rcn.com>

Printed and bound by Quebecor/Dubuque

Contents

Hi. I am Dr. Heidi.
My Little Scientists® friend Olivia and I are going to show you some interesting and fun experiments about water. Olivia loves the warm weather and the thing she likes best about it is water.

What is water?

Water is made up of very small molecules.
They are too small to be seen, but you can make a model
that will give you an idea of what a water molecule looks like.

You will need
- 2 grapes
- 1 plum or orange
- 2 toothpicks

1. Insert one toothpick into the top right and the other into the top left of the plum or orange. Place them at the points where you would expect teddy bear ears to be.

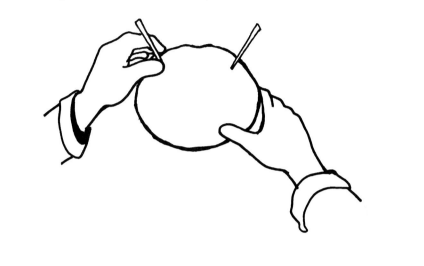

2. Push a grape onto each toothpick so that it now looks like a complete teddy bear head.

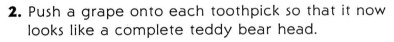

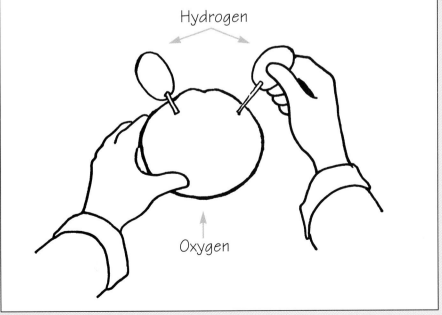

This is the shape of a water molecule. Millions and millions of very tiny molecules that look like this are in every drop of water!

How much of the Earth is covered with water?

More of the Earth is covered by water than land.
Water actually covers 75% of the Earth.
Let's do an experiment to better understand
what 3/4 of the Earth being covered with water means.

You will need
- 1/2 gallon clear plastic container
- 1 pint container
- 2 cups of sand
- 2 cups of water

1. Fill the pint container with sand and pour it into the clear 1/2 gallon container. (1/2 gallon is equal to four pints, so the container is now 1/4 full.)

2. Add 3 pints of water to the clear container.

This is just like the Earth's surface, which is 3/4 water and 1/4 land.

3. Now you can see that 3/4 of the clear container has water in it and only 1/4 has sand.

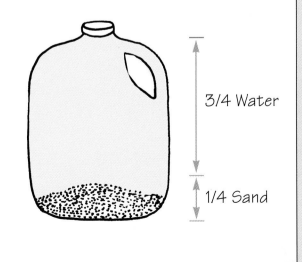

3/4 Water

1/4 Sand

Do I need water to live?

Water is very important for all living things. If there was no water on Earth, then there would be no life. This next experiment will show you how important water is for plants to grow and stay healthy.

You will need
- 3 plastic cups
- Package of marigold seeds
- Soil
- Water

1. Fill each cup almost full with soil.

2. Then plant three seeds in each cup according to the directions on the package.

3. Add water to two of the cups each day, but leave the third one dry.

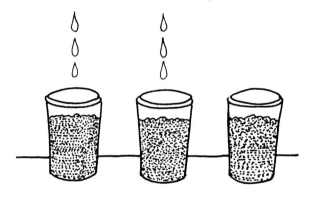

4. When plants start to grow, pick just one cup that you will water. From now on, leave the other two cups dry. Look at them every day. What happened? Which plants grew best?

Are water and ice
the same thing?

8

Water and ice are different forms of the same substance,
made up of the same molecules. This next experiment
will show how we can change water to ice and ice to water.

You will need
• 4 small
  paper cups
• Water
• 2 ice cubes
• Masking tape
• Marker
• A freezer

1. Label two cups "WATER" with a piece of masking tape and a marker.

2. Put water in the cups. Place one on the table and one in the freezer.

3. Label the remaining two cups "ICE" with a piece of masking tape and a marker.

4. Put one ice cube into each of the remaining cups. Place one on the table and one in the freezer.

5. After 2 hours, check the cups. What happened?

Ice is the solid form of water. Water is the liquid form. At room temperature,
water is in the liquid form. In the freezer, water is in the solid form called ice.
When water is taken from one temperature to the other, its form changes.
In this experiment you saw liquid water freeze and become ice. Ice taken out
of the freezer and left at room temperature melted and became liquid water.

Will this water stay cold all day? How will
I be able to drink this if it is frozen?

Ice is made of water molecules, but there are differences.
This experiment will help you discover how water changes when it freezes.

1. Fill the bottle with water almost to the top.

2. Mark the water line on the bottle with a permanent marker.

3. Stand the bottle up in the freezer.

4. Check back later in the day. Did the water freeze? Is the water still at the level you marked? What happened and why?

When water freezes, the molecules move apart a little as they attach to one another. This makes ice less dense than water and also explains why ice floats in water.

Why is the water colder
at the bottom than at the top?

Warm water floats on top of cold water. That is why the bottom of a lake feels colder. Let's do an experiment to prove this!

You will need
- 2 index cards (3" x 5")
- 4 clear plastic cups of the same size that can be covered completely by the index cards
- Ice cold water (enough to fill 2 of the cups)
- Hot water (enough to fill 2 of the cups)
- Red and blue food coloring
- Spoon

1. Fill two cups to the very top with hot water and the other two to the very top with cold water.

2. Add 2 or 3 drops of red coloring to the hot water. Then add 2 or 3 drops of blue coloring to the cold water. Stir each.

3. Place an index card over one cup of blue water. The index card should cover the mouth of the cup completely. Make sure to hold the card in place with the palm of one hand. Turn the cup upside down.

4. Now, place the upside-down blue water over the red water, carefully lining up the rims of the cups. Gently slide the card out and watch what happens.

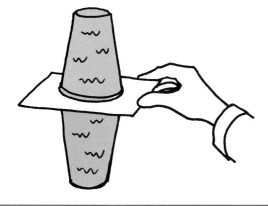

5. Now do it again, but this time put the red water over the blue water. Do you know why it behaved differently this time?

In step 4, the two colors mixed because the cold water immediately sank to the bottom. In step 5, the red water, which was warmer, floated on top and didn't mix with the colder blue water. The colder molecules are closer together and take up less space, making that water denser — (or heavier when you have an equal amount).

13

Which container has the most water?

Let's do an experiment to see if we can answer Olivia's question.

> **You will need**
> - 4 or more clear unbreakable containers of different shapes (e.g., syrup bottle, deli container, dish detergent bottle, honey jar, shampoo bottle)
> - Measuring cup for pouring
> - Water

1. Pour one cup of water into each of the containers.

2. Do they look like they have different amounts in them? What is the shape of the water in each jar?

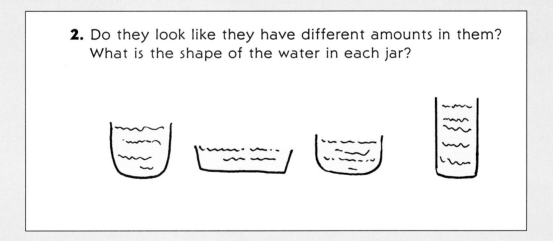

When the cup of water was poured into each container, the amount stayed the same but the water matched the shape of the container. If a container was shaped like a peanut, then the water inside would be shaped like a peanut, too! If the container was thinner, the water level was higher, but it was still the same amount of water. You can check this by pouring the water from each container, one at a time, back into the measuring cup.

Why is the water
level rising?

What Olivia is doing is called **displacement**.
The water level is changing, but is the amount of water changing?
If you do your own experiment, you will be able to discover the answer!

You will need
- Measuring cup
- 8-ounce cup
- Water
- Small rocks

1. Fill the measuring cup with water to the 4-ounce level.

2. Pour all the water into the larger cup.

3. Add rocks until the water level rises to the top of the cup.

4. Pour the water, but not the rocks, back into the measuring cup. Was there really more water after you added the rocks?

As the rocks were added, they pushed the water out of the way, so the water level got higher. It looked like there was more water, but when you poured it back into the measuring cup, you could see that the amount of water hadn't really changed.

What is keeping the water in the pail?

Surface tension is the name of what is keeping the water in Olivia's pail.
Water has a stronger surface tension than most other liquids.
Let's do an experiment to learn about the surface tension of water.

You will need
- Clear plastic cup
- Water
- Paper clips
- Pebbles
- Coins

1. Fill the cup with water until you see the dome of water on top that looks like the water in Olivia's bucket.

2. Carefully place one end of the paper clip in the middle of the dome and then let go. Keep adding the paper clips in this way, one at a time.

3. See how high the dome can go before it overflows. Try this experiment again with pebbles and then with coins.

The water molecules attract one another.
A water molecule in the middle of the cup is pulled equally in all directions.
Since there are no water molecules above the surface, the molecules at the surface
are pulled more closely together, allowing them to create the dome you observed.

Look at the shape of the water drops!

Surface tension also affects drops of water.
Let's do another experiment to see how.

You will need
- Medicine dropper
- Plastic plate
- Water
- Dime

1. Use the dropper to drip 3 or 4 drops of water onto the plate.

2. Notice how the drops stay in little domes rather than spreading out on the plate.

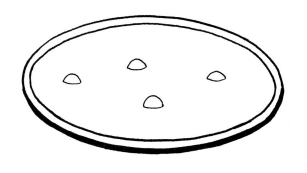

3. Now put one drop of water onto the dime. How many drops do you think you can put on the dime before it overflows?

4. Continue to add one drop at a time until it overflows. Was your prediction correct?

What is
keeping
the water
in the
little
spaces?

The answer to Olivia's question is surface tension — again!
However, you can do an even more interesting experiment that
uses surface tension and another force called **air pressure**.

You will need
- Glass jar
  (pint or quart)
- Piece of window
  screen mesh
  (6" x 6")
- Rubber band
- Water
- Sink

1. Cover the top of the jar with the piece of screen.

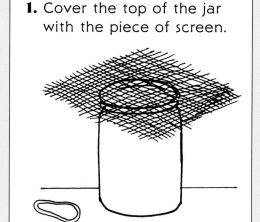

2. Use the rubber band to fasten the screen tightly in place.

3. Pour water through the screen until the jar is full.

4. Place your hand over the mouth of the jar and quickly turn it completely upside down over the sink.

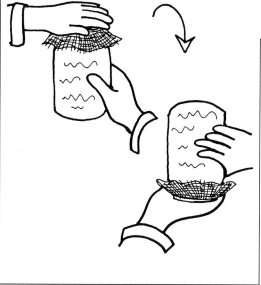

5. Remove your hand.

The water was pushing down, but air pressure was pushing up
and surface tension was holding the water in the holes of the screen.
As long as you held the mouth of the jar flat, the surface tension and
air pressure won. If you tilted the jar, however, water came pouring out!

23

What makes some things float on water and some things sink?

24

Things that are very light — such as a balloon — float. If you push them under water, they come right back up. Things that are very heavy — such as a rock — sink. Other things sometimes float and sometimes sink, depending on what is in them. In testing surface tension, you dropped paper clips into a cup and they sank. However, if you are careful, you can use surface tension to make a paper clip float! Let's do an experiment to learn more about floating.

You will need
• Bowl full of water
• Empty bowl
• Sink full of water
• Small rocks

1. Place both bowls into the sink full of water.

2. What happens?

3. Add rocks one at a time to the empty bowl.

4. What happens?

The empty bowl floats. When it gets too much water or too many rocks in it, it sinks. It has become too heavy for its size. That's why you don't want too many people in one boat!

How does a bubble hold together?

You know that bubbles are made of soap and water,
but did you know that the molecules are held together in a special way?

You will need
- Rectangular container
- Liquid dish detergent
- Measuring cup
- Water
- 2 straight drinking straws
- 36" string

1. Add one cup of liquid dish detergent and 4 cups of water to the container. Mix gently. Try not to make suds in the container.

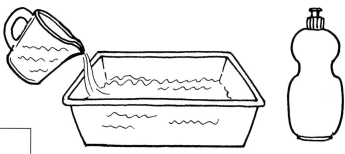

2. Loop the string through both straws and tie the ends of the string together.

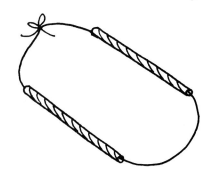

3. Spread the straws apart to make a rectangle.

4. Hold the middle of each straw. Dip the string and straws into the bubble solution.

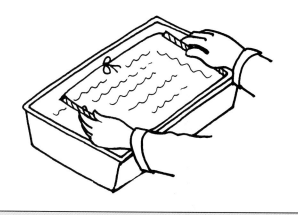

5. Lift it out. Observe the film that fills the inside of the rectangle.

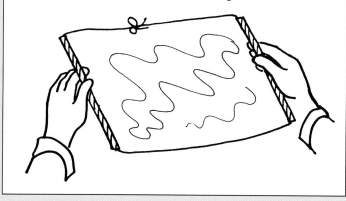

You have seen that water has an invisible "skin" on it caused by surface tension. The molecules in the bubble solution are also attracted to each other. The bubble solution molecules are long and stringy (like spaghetti). The bubble solution and water molecules hold together so well that they can make large areas of this skin or film. That's why bubbles hold together.

You can use objects of many shapes to blow bubbles and the bubbles will still be round. Try this experiment to see for yourself. Each item you choose must have a rim or sides all around, so that the soap and water solution is able to form a film.

You will need
- Bubble solution
- Metal can with both ends removed
- Plastic rings from a six-pack of soda
- Mesh strawberry basket
- Pipe cleaner bent into any shape ring you like
- Paper cup with the bottom cut out

1. Dip one item into the bubble solution as made in the previous activity.

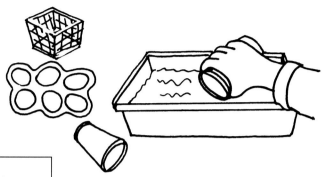

2. Make bubbles by gently waving the item through the air.

3. Repeat this with each other item.

4. Which items make large bubbles? Which make small bubbles?

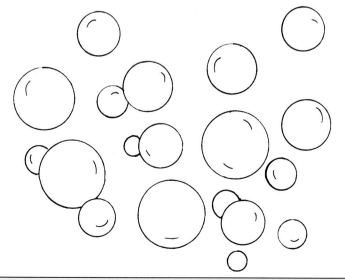

5. Which items make bubbles one at a time? Which make several at a time?

The bubble solution in the bubble is trying to come together while the air inside the bubble is pushing out.

The round shape lets the solution get as close together as possible!

I can stick my finger right into this bubble and it doesn't break!

We can see why Olivia's bubble didn't break
by using something stronger than a bubble.

You will need
• Sealable
  plastic bag
• Water
• Sharp pencil
• Sink

1. Hold the plastic bag in the sink
and fill it with water.

2. Seal the bag.

3. Hold the bag by the sealed edge with one hand.
With your other hand push the pencil in one side and
then through the other side, keeping the pencil level.

4. Notice that the bag does
not leak even though
there are two holes in it.

5. Keeping the bag over the sink,
remove the pencil.

The plastic bag didn't leak water when it was poked, just as the bubble
didn't leak air when Olivia poked her finger through it. This is because the
molecules in both the plastic and the bubble moved aside to let the object through and
then quickly moved back around the pencil or finger to seal the opening.

Can we make bubbles last long enough to catch them?

You made bubbles using soap and water.
Would the bubbles last longer if we used more detergent or less detergent?
What would happen if we added other ingredients?
Let's experiment to find out how to make the longest lasting bubbles!

You will need
- Water
- Liquid dish detergent
- Bowl
- Tablespoon
- Cups
- Bubble wand
- Glycerin
  (from a pharmacy)
- Teaspoon
- Sugar
- Salt
- Watch with a second hand
- Other ingredients —
  use your imagination

1. Put one tablespoon of liquid dish detergent and three tablespoons of water in a cup.

2. Dip the bubble wand into the solution and blow a bubble. Use the watch to see how long it lasts before it pops. Do this at least two or three times.

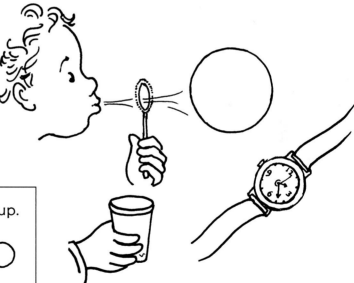

3. Add a teaspoon of glycerin to the cup. Blow a new set of bubbles and see how long each one lasts.

4. Repeat steps 1-3, but use sugar in place of glycerin.

5. Repeat this experiment trying salt and other ingredients. Try changing the amount of liquid dish detergent you use, too.

Where does rain come from?

Rain comes from the clouds, but that is not the entire story.
Would you like to make rain in a fish bowl?

You will need
- Help from an adult
- One-gallon fish bowl
- Plastic sandwich bag
- Rubber band
- Ice
- Very hot water

1. Have an adult pour some very hot water into the fish bowl.

2. Placing the sandwich bag partially inside the fish bowl, flip the edge around the rim of the fish bowl.

3. Use the rubber band to firmly attach the bag to the fish bowl.

4. Place several ice cubes inside the sandwich bag. They should be hanging inside the fish bowl.

5. Watch to see what happens inside the fish bowl.

You only see a small number of rain drops because this is a very small cloud!

When water in oceans, lakes and rivers evaporates, water **vapor** rises. As it cools, it forms clouds.

When the clouds get too heavy or they touch cold air, water vapor condenses into liquid water and falls back to the ground, oceans, lakes, and rivers in the form of rain or snow.

This happens all the time, over and over again. This is called the **water cycle**.

Why do crackers sometimes get soft and mushy?

Fresh crackers and cereal can get soft and mushy
when they are left out of their packages.
Let's do an experiment to discover why.

You will need
- 3 cereal bowls
- Cup of dry cereal (corn flakes works very well)
- Water
- Measuring cup

1. Put 1/4 cup of dry cereal in a bowl and leave it on the table overnight.

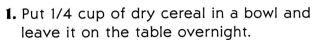

2. The next morning, pour a 1/4 cup of new cereal into another bowl.

3. Taste them both. How are they different? What has happened to the cereal that was left overnight?

4. Next put 1/4 cup of cereal in the third bowl and add 1/4 cup of water.

5. Compare it to the cereal you left out overnight. You can leave the cereal that you left overnight for another night to see if it gets even softer or you can give it to the birds.

Cereal and crackers can take in water from the air. This is called **absorption**.
The water is what makes them softer.

Why does water sometimes disappear?

38

Let's try to find out why water sometimes disappears.

You will need
- Small, plastic plate
- Water
- Sunny window
- Teaspoon
- Kitchen timer

1. Put the plastic plate in the sun near a window.

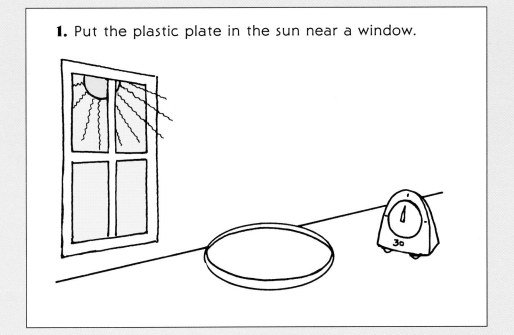

2. Use the teaspoon to put some water on the plate. Make a small puddle of water and a few separate drops.

3. Check it every 30 minutes.

The water will gradually disappear. This is called **evaporation**.
Water molecules escape into the air one at a time. They are too small to see,
but we can notice the change over time.

Where did the water on the outside of this can come from?

When you let cold things sit for a little time, water appears on the surface.
Let's test to understand why this happens.

You will need
- Empty metal can
  (a coffee can works well)
- Ice cubes

1. Fill the metal can with ice cubes.

2. Put it in a warm place and
leave it for a few minutes.

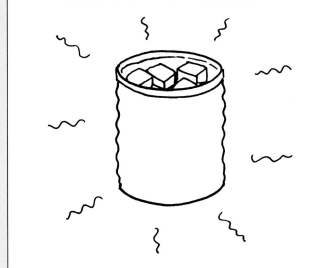

3. Take a look at the container
and see what's on the outside.

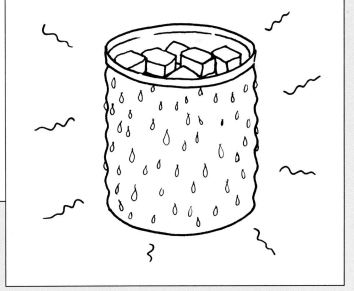

You will see drops of water have formed. This is called **condensation**.
Just as water can evaporate into the air, it can also come back out of the air!
When water vapor in the air comes in contact with the can, the water changes
from a gas (water vapor) to a liquid form (water drops) because the can is very cold.

Which way
does water flow?

Let's do an experiment to find out how water flows.

You will need
• Flat pan or cookie sheet
• Sink
• Water faucet

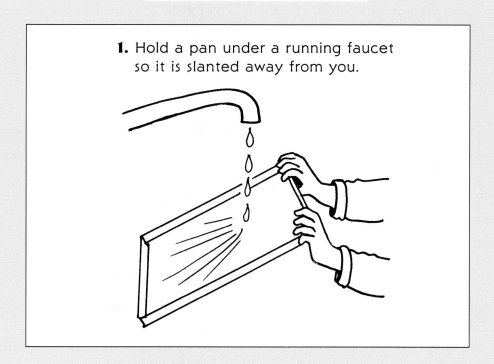

1. Hold a pan under a running faucet so it is slanted away from you.

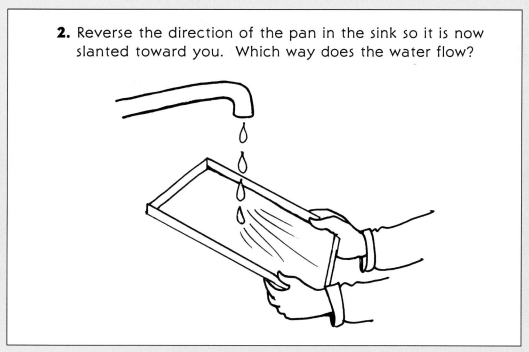

2. Reverse the direction of the pan in the sink so it is now slanted toward you. Which way does the water flow?

Water always flows downhill.
The water is pulled downhill by a force called **gravity**.

What can flowing water do?

Water goes downhill, but does it change the hill?
Let's find out by doing another experiment.

You will need
- Large, disposable tray
  (or you can do this outside)
- Clay
- Dirt
- Sand
- Pieces of plants and twigs
- Plastic bowl
- Container with water in it

1. Build a land model by pressing lumps of clay on the tray to represent the solid rock underneath the ground.

2. Cover the tray and clay, first with a layer of dry dirt and then with a layer of dry sand.

3. Use twigs and small parts of plants to represent trees and bushes.

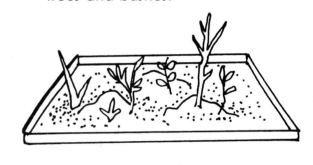

4. To form a slope, place the plastic bowl upside down under one end of the tray.

5. Pour water from the container onto the highest edge of the tray. Where did the rivers form? What happened to the dirt and sand?

What you have seen is called **erosion**.
This is how flowing water forms streams and rivers and wears away the land.

While some things dissolve in water, others don't.
Let's experiment to see what things do mix with water and what things do not.

You will need
- Water
- Pepper
- Salt
- Sugar
- Sand
- 8-ounce clear plastic cups
- Spoons

1. Fill one cup with water half full.

2. Add a spoonful of salt to the cup and stir with the spoon. What happens?

3. Add a spoonful of pepper to another cup of water and stir with the spoon. What happens?

4. Add each of the other ingredients to a separate cup of water and stir in the same way to see what happens.

Some things mix or dissolve in water and some things do not.
Those that mix are called **soluble**. Those that do not mix are called **insoluble**.

Where did the water go
that we mixed with the gelatin?

Sometimes water combines with other substances.
Water molecules are still there, but we can't see them.

You will need
- Help from an adult
- Package of your favorite flavor gelatin
- 1 cup of very hot water
- 1 cup of very cold water
- Bowl
- Spoon
- Refrigerator

1. Have an adult heat up the water according to the directions on the packet of gelatin and pour the hot water into the bowl.

2. Dissolve the gelatin in the hot water, stirring them together with a spoon.

3. Add the cold water and mix with the spoon.

4. Put the bowl of gelatin in the refrigerator to set.

5. Check in a few hours. Where is the water? What happened?

The water molecules have attached to the gelatin molecules.
They are still present, but they are in a different form.

How did the ice change the juice?

What Olivia has observed is another example of displacement.
Let's do an experiment to see if you can answer Olivia's questions.

You will need
- Disposable clear plastic cup
- Food coloring
- 2 ice cubes
- Water
- Permanent marker

1. Fill the cup about half full with water.

2. Add a few drops of food coloring.

3. Mark the level with a permanent marker. What do you think will happen to the level of the water when you add ice?

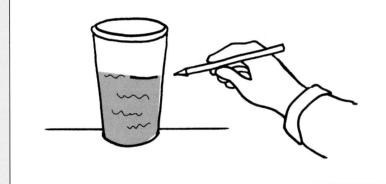

4. Add two ice cubes. Mark the new level.

5. Look at the level of the colored water when the ice has melted.

The amount of ice above the level of the colored water matches the **volume** of water in the ice.

Why does the water
spray that way?

52

The water molecules are attracted to each other and stick together as they flow off the spoon. Let's test how this changes using different surfaces.

You will need
- Large spoon
- Sink faucet
- Drinking straw
- Twelve-inch piece of rope
- String of beads

1. Hold the spoon upside down at a downward angle over the sink.

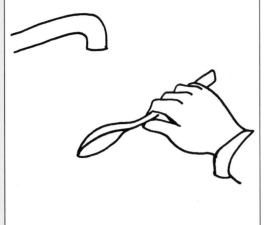

2. Let water from the faucet run over the spoon.

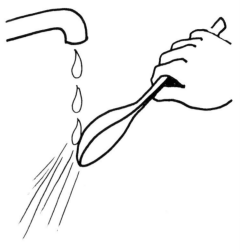

3. Next, hold the drinking straw at an angle. Try running water slowly down the drinking straw. What happens to the water falling on the straw?

4. Try this again with a piece of rope and a string of beads.

The sheet of water formed because of the attraction of water molecules to each other. The water followed the spoon before spilling into the sink. The water molecules also should have followed each other down the straw or any other surface.

Why is the water squirting up?

Let's find out why water shoots out of a bottle when we squeeze it!

You will need
• Empty plastic water bottle
• Water
• Sink

1. Fill an empty water bottle about 3/4 full.

2. Hold it over the sink. Squeeze the bottle. What happened to the water?

As you squeezed the water bottle, you displaced the area where the water had been. The water molecules couldn't move closer together, so they had to move upward and out of the bottle!

Olivia has thought a lot
about water today!

Glossary

absorption — taking water into something

air pressure — a force of air molecules pushing against everything they touch

attraction — two substances or particles pulling one another together

compression — forcing something into a smaller volume

condensation — water molecules in the air gathering on a surface and becoming liquid water

displacement — moving something aside and replacing it

erosion — wearing away soil or dirt

evaporation — gradually changing from a liquid to a gas

gas — the form of a substance which matches the shape and volume of its container

gravity — a force that pulls things down to Earth

insoluble — will not mix when placed in a second substance, for example, marbles in water

liquid — the form of a substance which has a constant volume but matches the shape of the container

molecule — the smallest part of a substance

solid — the form of a substance which has a constant volume and shape

soluble — will mix when placed in a second substance, for example, sugar in water

surface tension — an attractive force between the molecules at the surface of a liquid

vapor — liquid molecules floating in a gas

volume — the amount of space occupied by something

water cycle — the continuous movement of water back and forth between the ground and the air including evaporation, condensation, and precipitation (rain and snow)

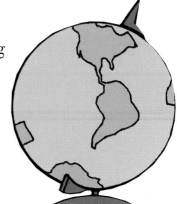